THE
Invincible
GOD

Unconquerable *and* Undefeatable

REBEKAH POWELL

Copyright © 2014 Rebekah Powell.

All rights reserved. No part of this book may be reproduced, stored, or transmitted by any means—whether auditory, graphic, mechanical, or electronic—without written permission of both publisher and author, except in the case of brief excerpts used in critical articles and reviews. Unauthorized reproduction of any part of this work is illegal and is punishable by law.

Unless otherwise noted, all scripture quotations are from the New King James Version. Copyright 1979, 1980, 1982 by Thomas Nelson, Inc., publishers. Used by permission. Amplified Bible Version

Scripture quotations identified AMP are from the Amplified Bible, copyright 1954, 1958, 1962, 1964, 1965, 1987 by The Lockman Foundation. Used by permission.

ISBN: 978-0-615-95636-7 (sc)
ISBN: 978-1-4834-0771-5 (e)

Because of the dynamic nature of the Internet, any web addresses or links contained in this book may have changed since publication and may no longer be valid. The views expressed in this work are solely those of the author and do not necessarily reflect the views of the publisher, and the publisher hereby disclaims any responsibility for them.

Any people depicted in stock imagery provided by Thinkstock are models, and such images are being used for illustrative purposes only.
Certain stock imagery © Thinkstock.

Lulu Publishing Services rev. date: 03/06/2014

Dedication

I joyfully dedicate this book to Holy Spirit who has entrusted and guided me in the completion of this book. I thank my loving husband, Jermaine, who is my confidant and truly emboldens me. I thank my beautiful children, Timothy and Lydia, for teaching me so much about patience and perseverance.

Contents

Foreword ix
Acknowledgments xi

Introduction xiii
Chapter 1   The Infallible Hero 1
Chapter 2   The Almighty God is Truly an Invincible Warrior ... 6
Chapter 3   We Are Not Born to Live Confused and Lost 11
Chapter 4   The Mighty Warrior 20
Chapter 5   How Do You See God? 26
Chapter 6   God's Infinite Thoughts toward His People 33
Chapter 7   Our Obedience to the Mighty Warrior Gives
              Us Victory 37
Chapter 8   The Splendor of God 40
Chapter 9   Trust in the Invincible God—No Matter
              What Happens 43
Chapter 10 Access to the Invincible God through Christ Jesus .. 55

Personal Testimonies of God Ministering through Me in
    Prophetic Songs 59
Recommended Reading 67
Notes 71
About IFOC 73

Foreword

The very exquisite Holy Spirit inspired this writing. It is vital to the believer and the unbeliever. It is a book that is very practical. Rebekah's transparency helps reveal reality and the simplicity of who God is. We can talk to God, express, and confess with our hearts. He is there and will always be there.

This book shows the diverse attributes of God's character and love, as a warrior, priest, and king. Whatever it is, there are no limitations with God. I thank God for my beautiful queen and wonderful mother to our two children, Lydia and Timothy, and her obedience to the Holy Spirit to write an inspiring, life-giving testimony of who and what God can be in our lives when we trust in him. This is an awesome book!

—Jermaine Powell

"For you are the God who performs miracles; you display your power among the peoples."
—Psalm 77:14

Acknowledgments

I give thanks to my loving and giving parents, Jerry and Irene Matthews, who raised and taught the Word of God to their fourteen children. I love, respect, and honor them as my parents. I thank my loving apostles, Alvin and Alva Green, for their spiritual guidance, love, and support. I love, respect, and honor them as spiritual parents.

I am thankful for all the special individuals who have improved my life through their precious time, words of wisdom, books, financial gifts, teachings, and fervent prayers. I appreciate all those who worked diligently in helping to publish this book.

Introduction

The Invincible God was inspired through me by the Holy Spirit on April 8, 2011. While resting on my bed, the words "invincible God" came to me in the image of a book. I immediately began to write as the words came. The Lord began giving me scriptures that would display his invincibility as the almighty God.

I must say that an excitement came over me immediately because I have grown to see the Lord as the mighty warrior that he is. Through the years of my intimate relationship with him, he has always been my mighty warrior. I'm crazy in love with him, and I am blown away by his perfect love. It is a privilege to embrace and honor my relationship with such an awesome, magnificent warrior. His pure, unique love is abounding abundantly for me. Each day is an opportunity to discover the limitless possibilities with my mighty warrior. Each day is a challenging journey to experience, but it is well worth it because I serve an invincible God.

I wouldn't be where I am today if not for my biological parents. I thank them for giving my siblings and me the chance to live life. I thank them for doing their best at parenting and for the many sacrifices made while raising fourteen children of their own. I know it wasn't easy for them, but God was with them all the time. My parents were blessed with eight handsome sons and six beautiful daughters. We didn't attend a regular Sunday service gathering.

My parents taught us about the Word of God. We would have church right in our home. Many churchgoing people who knew my parents didn't speak too well of my parents because of this. Some people didn't consider them to be believers of Christ Jesus either. My parents didn't let this stop them from having Bible study in their home. On a few occasions, some of us would accompany my grandmother and one of my aunts to a church service. My parents planted the seed of Christ in me as a child, and others helped water it.

I accepted Christ Jesus as my personal Lord and savior at the age of fourteen. A friend of mine asked me to accompany her to a church revival. I didn't want to go at first because I thought it would be boring. After much thought, I decided I would go. The guest speaker painted a very clear picture about what would happen if you died that night and didn't know Jesus. The speaker asked one simple question, "Does Jesus know you?" I thought deeply for a few minutes.

I thought about how I had been taught about God, Jesus, and the Holy Spirit, but I did not have a relationship with the Lord. I felt a strong tugging within that was impossible to ignore. The next thing I knew, I was up and walking toward the altar with tears in my eyes. I remember saying quietly to the Lord that I wanted to know him. That was how my journey with the Lord began.

I would read the Bible in bed at night. I had a difficult time understanding much of what I read in the scriptures. One night, I closed the Bible in frustration. With tears in my eyes, I looked up toward the heavens and asked, "God, how am I supposed to know you if I don't understand what I'm reading?" I turned off the lights and cried myself to sleep.

When I was seventeen, I received the Holy Spirit and my prayer language. I was living in Hawaii, and it was seventeen years ago. It was a significant experience in my life.

After receiving the Holy Spirit, I was able to have a clearer understanding of the Word of God. The more I read it, the more I wanted to see it in operation. In many of the churches I visited, I was surprised to find a one-man show or a pastor-and-wife show. There were also many religious programs that were nonstop for the purpose of man praise and entertainment. The spirit of religion is in full effect in many of churches today, and it has crippled many in the body of Christ. The spirit of religion is an ancient spirit.

While I was praying one day, the Lord shared his thoughts about religion with me. The truth about religion is that it smothers the very life out of people. The spirit of religion kills, and God hates it.

God said, "I want to add and build not detest (dislike intensely). I'm building and restoring my people, not killing them with religion. Religion is not of me. I hate religion, and I despise it. One can't grow into full maturity in religion; it stunts all growth. I'm not of it; it's not me. I very much dislike it. It is distasteful in my sight. I see it as straight bondage. It quenches my spirit from moving beyond where I want it to go. It stops me from ministering to my people what I want them to hear and know. It stops all flow of revelation from heaven. It kills and destroys my people. I hate it; it is distasteful in my sight. My presence wants to pour it out and devour it all up to be no more, but I have instilled those on the earth to tear down the spirit of religion."

The good news is that the invincible God is restoring his Church back to its original glorified kingdom position. The Church (God's people) is the beautiful bride of Christ without spots or wrinkles.

The purpose of this book is to express the heart and mind of God. He desires for all to know him as the invincible God that he is. He searches for those who will believe in him, trust in him, and worship him. He takes pleasure in our faith in him. To have faith in God means we have confidence in him to be who he says he is. Throughout the entire Bible, scriptures reveal the very essence of who he is. He has even revealed himself through divine names such as Alpha and Omega, the beginning and the end, El Shaddai the all-sufficient one (the God who is more than enough), and Jehovah Shalom—the Lord is my peace. These are only a few of his many names; others are mentioned in chapter 5.

There is an abundance of revelation to be poured out about God and his kingdom. This divine revelation is not given for private interpretation. It is not given for our egos or selfish gain. God releases it for a divine purpose that is paramount for kingdom advancement. The earthly life that we embark on is not all about us. It is all about the kingdom of God.

Heaven does not function and operate like the worldly system we live in. God has something much greater in mind that involves the Church. I know that the kingdom of God is within me. I don't have to wait until I enter heaven to experience the kingdom of God.

There is evidence of God's true existence all around us, but it's up to each individual to decide whether he or she wants to believe, accept, and trust in the Lord. We all will see God face-to-face one day. We all will bow down and confess with our very own tongue that he is Lord. We all will live for eternity as spirit beings after our physical bodies die. However, not all will live eternally with the invincible God and his son, Christ Jesus. The time is now for all to know and see God as the invincible warrior in life and to build an everlasting relationship with him.

Chapter One

The Infallible Hero

Many people, young and old, are searching for someone to look up to, believe in, and trust. There is nothing wrong with having a positive role model to help inspire you, like a child choosing his or her favorite superhero, the hero that can do the impossible and the incredible. It does not matter what the circumstance are; he is superb for a child. The Creator of heaven and earth can do the impossible, the incredible, and the miraculous, no matter what the circumstances are. We all have our weaknesses and strengths as humans; this is nothing new to the Creator. God made us this way, and that is why he is the infallible one and we are not.

I see people looking for a superhero to solve all their problems. Who are those fallible heroes that many seek? They include presidents, governors, mayors, senators, pastors, counselors, parents, teachers, mentors, brothers, sisters, aunts, uncles, celebrities, and friends. An earthly hero will always have fleshly weaknesses and strengths that will prohibit him or her from being invincible.

Faith is for anyone who wants to know, believe, and see God as invincible, a mighty, unstoppable warrior who is unconquerable and undefeatable. When we believe, have faith (total confidence) in God, and apply his divine principles to life, we accomplish our desires and goals. Delight yourself in the Lord, and he will give you the desires of your heart.

To delight yourself in the Lord is to seek or search out what pleases God. How do we find out what pleases him? Proverbs 4:7 says that wisdom is the principle thing, and Deuteronomy 4:6 says that wisdom is the law of God applied to solve our problems.

Matthew 6:33 tells us to seek first the kingdom of heaven and all its righteousness, and these things shall be added to you. The Word of God can solve any problem. We tend to think that we have all the answers, but we forget that this is our first time on earth. We certainly did not create ourselves. Therefore, it is God's desire for us to believe and have faith in him for who he is. It grieves him to see people suffer in ignorance because they simply don't have enough confidence in him to apply his divine principles.

God Stands by His Words

I don't presume to think I know everything, but I do consider myself a personal witness to him as the one and only invincible God. After taking a college class about world religion, I understand why people are so confused and lost in the world. We were not born to be confused and lost about our identities. We were created by a true divine Creator with a divine purpose and plan for our lives. There is no other like him, and there will never be any other like him. What god is as great as God? The answer is none.

"For you are the God who performs miracles; you display your power among the peoples" (Psalm 77:14). He is the only God who can show forth great miracles. I love to boast about God and his infinite wisdom. It is impossible for me not to boast about him. God is wise, strong, powerful, omnipotent, omnipresent, and righteous. You can always count on God to come through for you. He will always stand by his words. In life, it's not all about what a person says he or she will do. It all comes down to what a person can and will do after stating it.

I have found myself in some sticky situations that almost always look hopeless from a faithless perspective. The key thing that I zoom in on to help me persevere is the fact that God, also known as Yahweh, has never failed me and will never lie to me. Therefore, I can always count on my invincible warrior. There were times I cried myself to sleep because things didn't turn out as I had hoped they would. Later, I realized that the situations somehow worked to my advantage. Nevertheless, I will always trust in the Creator because God always backs up his words.

God Wants Us Closer to Him

This is a true statement that I'm about to make. There are individuals in my life that I respect and love dearly and have known for years, but I still don't have a solid relationship with them. They have set boundaries for how close I can get, and I will not force myself beyond those boundaries. Therefore, the relationship really never grows to another level. It stays fragile and shallow. I know more about God than I know about them. Why is that? God doesn't mind me getting close to him. I believe that God truly wants me to have a real, solid relationship with him. God wants us to be closer to him. As we draw closer to God, he reveals more and more of himself to us. This comes from worshipping only him, spending time in prayer, reading and meditating on the Word of God, singing songs of praise, and fasting.

The closer we get, the more we learn how to think like him. I want to think like God does. As believers, we transform our minds by reading and applying the Word of God daily. We know that humans are made up of a body, soul, and spirit. The body is a natural covering for the soul and the spirit.

The soul consists of the emotions, mind, and will. When we receive Jesus Christ as our personal savior, our spirit awakens to life. We pray for the Holy Spirit to come and dwell within our spirit. Reading the Bible, praying in the spirit, fasting, and applying the Word of God daily helps our spirit grow strong and healthy.

God wants the spirit to rule over the mind and soul. We should want this as well. This is necessary if we want to live an abundant life through Christ. Although we are here on earth, the kingdom way is a much better way for us to live. God's kingdom principles are marrow to our bones and strength to our joints. The wisdom of God is his Word. God has given us everything we need to transform our minds. We have to want to change our thinking if we are going to think like God does. It is an extraordinary honor and privilege to have a personal relationship with God, especially since he is omnipresent and omnipotent.

For Review

- Define faith.
- Do you have a relationship with God? If so, is the relationship healthy?
- Explain what it means to think like God. Why is it necessary for us to transform our minds?

- We know that humans are made up of a body, soul, and spirit. Our body is a natural covering for our soul and our spirit. What do the soul consist of? Define the difference between soul and spirit.
- God want us to draw closer and closer to him, and he reveals more and more of himself to us. Explain how we can draw closer to God. How does he reveal himself to us?

Chapter Two

The Almighty God is Truly an Invincible Warrior

The almighty God is truly an invincible warrior. The scriptures give countless details about his glorious testimonies. The way he moves with his spirit and shows his splendor throughout the land is marvelous to behold.

I love to reflect on how God uses his divine, flawless strategies when going into battle. I am reminded of Habakkuk 3:19, which speaks of God being an invincible army. The Lord God is my strength, my personal bravery, and my invincible army. He makes my feet like hinds' feet and will make me to walk (not to stand still in terror, but to walk) and make (spiritual) progress upon my high places (of trouble, suffering, or responsibility). "With God rests my salvation and my glory; He is my Rock of unyielding strength and impenetrable hardness, and my refuge is in God!" The Word of God teaches us to trust in, lean on, rely on, and have confidence in him at all times. Pour out your hearts before him. God is a refuge for us. A fortress and a high tower (Psalm 62:7, 8 AMP). There is safety and strength in God.

What It Means to Be Invincible

Let's get a better understanding of what it means to be invincible. According to the *Collins English Dictionary*, *invincible* (ɪnˈvɪnsəbᵉl) is an adjective meaning "incapable of being defeated; unconquerable, unable to be overcome; insuperable (from Late Latin *invincibilis*, from Latin IN-¹ + *vincere* to conquer)."

Here are similar words to describe its meaning:

- *Unassailable*—impossible to dispute or disprove; undeniable and not subject to attack or seizure
- *Indestructible*—incapable of being destroyed, ruined, or rendered ineffective
- *Impregnable*—unable to be broken into or taken by force; unable to be shaken; overcome and incapable of being refuted
- *Insuperable*—impossible of being surmounted or excelled
- *Invulnerable*—immune to attack, unconquerable (not capable of being conquered, vanquished, or overcome)
- *Insurmountable*—not capable of being surmounted or overcome
- *Indomitable*—impossible to frighten, subdue, or defeat
- *Unyielding*—not bending; inflexible; not giving way to pressure or persuasion; obdurate

The opposite of invincible is "weak, vulnerable, powerless, yielding, unprotected, defenseless, beatable, assailable, and conquerable" (*Collins Thesaurus of the English Language*). Of course, the true living God has none of these characteristics.

Lord of Armies

There are numerous scriptures in the bible that will reveal God as the only true invincible warrior also known as Yahweh Sabaoth, "Lord of Armies". God's army includes the angelic host, the physical heavens and the church. I will be focusing on the scriptures that I believe the Lord gave me on the night of June 29th 2011. Let us witness His miraculous power and faithfulness as an invincible God. The Old Testament book of Joshua reads of the miraculous acts that took place in Gibeon a city of the Hivites. In Joshua 10:11-13 the Lord cast great hail stones from the heavens on the enemies of Israel. There were more people who died from the hail stone that day than the Israelites slew with their sword. The sun stood still in the sky and the moon stayed in its place for the whole day during Joshua's battle with the five confederate kings. God used the Red Sea to over throw pharaoh and his army. These miraculous acts were done so that the Israelites would conquer and defeat their enemies the Amorites upon the Lords command. Here we can vividly see God use the physical heavens as weapons to help the Israelites defeat their enemy.

Only the creator of the creation can perform such and act. God created the sun by speaking it into existence. He created man by speaking and making us in His own image. We as human beings must know that we did not create ourselves and that we didn't evolve from monkeys. Therefore we need to acknowledge that there is a higher greater supreme deity that lives and governs over the universe that we call earth. When we come to the realization of this and accept it for what it is; we then give ourselves the liberty to search out the word of God and go on an enlighten, amazing, exciting and challenging journey with the mighty warrior. In acknowledging Him we then give ourselves the liberty to accept

Him as the supreme God of the universe and desire to learn and discover all that we can about Him.

The Lord helps Gideon fight the Midianites with only 300 soldiers

In the book of Judges chapter seven verse seven it tells how Gideon a warrior of the Lord fought the Midianites with only 300 soldiers. The Lord helped Gideon fight the Midianites with only 300 soldiers so that Gideon and his army would know that it was truly the Lord God Almighty and not them alone.

The Lord delivers the Philistines into David's hands

In 2 Samuel 5:23-24 the Lord delivers the Philistines into David's hands in an unusual way. This particular battle began when the Philistines heard that David had been anointed king over Israel. Then the Philistines came after David. When David found out that the Philistines were near he went to the key source for guidance. David went to the Lord and asked if it was good to go confront his enemy the Philistines. David gets permission and divine instructions from the Lord. The Lord instructs David not to go up as he had planned, but to go around behind the Philistines and seize upon them opposite the mulberry trees. David and his men are to wait on the Lords signal. They are to listening for the sound of marching in the tops of the mulberry trees. The marching sound of numerous soldiers by the mulberry trees would lead the Philistines right into the hands of David. The Lord of armies had went ahead of them and overtaken the Philistines.

The Lord opened the servant's eyes to see the heavens chariots

In the book of 2 kings 6:15-17 God reveals and demonstrates His infamous invincibility of power and protection to the servant of Elisha the prophet. It happened when the king of Syria was warring against Israel, Elisha the prophet informed the king of Israel of the Syrians secret plan. This angered the king of Syria and he sent forth horses, chariots and a great army so that they might seize Elisha in the city of Dothan. When the servant of Elisha rose up early in the morning, behold an army with horses and chariots were around the city. Then Elisha's servant asked him what are we to do? Elisha said, "fear not; for those with us are more than those with them". Elisha prayed and asked God to open the eyes of the young man, so that he may see the mountain was full of horses and chariots of fire round about Elisha. The Lord did as Elisha asked and when the eyes of the servant were opened he saw the mountains full of horses and chariots of fire all around Elisha.

For Review

- Explain what Yahweh Sabaoth means. Be specific.
- What are some physical elements the Lord used to help the Israelites defeat their enemies?
- Why did David go to the Lord to ask if it was good to confront his enemy (the Philistines)?
- Why did Elisha pray and ask God to open the eyes of the young man?

Chapter Three

We Are Not Born to Live Confused and Lost

Throughout the world, there are hurting people who have placed their trust in the hands of others or some form of false deity. Many people are taught early in childhood what they should believe, but others choose to believe in what they want. Many people believe in the Tooth Fairy, Santa Claus, tiny elves, boogie monsters, good witches, and bad witches. Some people even believe in Greek myths, old superstitious fables, black magic, voodoo, and ancestral spirit guides. People around the world actually believe in these things, but when I ask them if they believe in God, they say "no," "I think so," "maybe," "yes," or "I don't know."

Many people have placed their trust in the hands of others and are expecting the miraculous to happen. When these miracles do not happen, they are crushed to the core even more than before. Some people reach out for love and compassion or feel as though they have nowhere to go. All the while, God was right there, waiting to be believed in and trusted. God wants us to have faith in him. When we have faith in him, we have confidence in him. We have confidence that he is able to do exactly what he said he would do. The truth of our faith is our expectation in him. God takes pleasure in our expectations of him because it requires faith.

"But without faith, it is impossible to please him: for he that cometh to God must believe that he is and that he is a reward of them that diligently seek him" (Hebrews 11:6). We can see that God takes great joy when we believe in him, but there is no joy when we doubt him.

I am so in love with God and know him as the invincible God because every time I have believed and expected him to move on my behalf, he has never failed me. He is always supportive of me—even when I have made a wrong decision. God has never called me stupid, dumb, insignificant, or any other degrading names. Why would he when God created me? Of course, there are times I have acted quickly and made poor decisions that resulted in pain. My decision may have been stupid, but it does not mean that I am stupid. We all will do something in life that will make us feel dumb, but God does not see us like this. He knows we don't know everything, but we think we do. We seem to think we understand everything about life, but we don't know everything. God is near us, waiting for us to believe and reach out to him. This is one reason I believe God has great mercy and patience toward us.

Your Greatest Discovery in Life

There were times when I didn't have a clue about what I was supposed to do. The individuals around me were gossiping about me instead of trying to help me. There were times when people treated me as though I was insignificant. Does this still happen? Of course it does. The one person I would always turn to is God. I would read and listen to what the Creator said I was and what he said I was purposed for. I haven't been on earth too long, but I have been here long enough to know that life is not fair or easy. I've discovered that many things must be learned, endured, and overcome in order to enjoy life. I have come to learn that my happiness determines my success in life. Life is not about competing against everyone else or living out someone else's lost dreams. It's about living a life of purpose and meaning to the promises of God. We are to live a life of abundance in God.

Your greatest discovery in life is to discover who you are and know your purpose here on earth. God has given each of us a purpose and has equipped us with the tools needed to accomplish it. I desire to complete everything God intended for me to accomplish for him. It brings me great joy to do things that please God. I like nice things and new things, but I don't take pride in material items. Having many items will not bring inner peace to your life. When a person is only after earthly possessions and self-gratification, there will still be an empty void present. Why is there an empty void? Why is there no peace to be found within? Remember that our greatest discovery in life is to really know who we are and know our purpose for being here on earth. When we discover this, it is not for us to rush in it. We must embrace it and take it day by day.

God Loves Simplicity

I am after the heart of God. The things that excite me the most in life are not of this world. The world makes things complicated, but God makes things simple. I am after what pleases God. I desire to have and operate in God's wisdom. I remember when my husband

and I attended a prophet conference in North Carolina. We were good friends at the time, and we both were a part of the singles ministry at our church. We were so excited and nervous at the same time. During one session, a group of us were teamed up.

My husband teamed up with me, and two other people in leadership joined us. They began to explain the prophetic exercise and then prayed for us. After they had spoken and released what God had given them concerning us, we were to speak and release what we believed God was giving us concerning them. This was considered a challenge for us, and we were very nervous.

We prayed and explained what we had seen and heard from God. When we finished, one of the leaders told us that God was pleased with our simplicity. God loves simplicity. We had only released what we had seen and heard. We didn't try to add anything to it or leave anything out. I will always remember that because it gave me great insight and peace with God. I have seen many Christians who want to make it seem difficult to come to God. Some people don't know anything about God or have the wrong impressions about God.

Many people think living for God is only about doing work. This is nothing more than religion. There is a distinctive difference between having a form of religion and having a relationship with the Lord. Many believe that doing a whole lot of so-called good things will get them closer to God and right into heaven, but it won't. What they fail to realize is that God wants to have a personal, intimate relationship with them. There are millions of people doing good things on earth, but the sad part is that they don't have the personal testimony of Christ Jesus and a personal relationship with God. Every year, millions of people across the world celebrate Christmas. This major holiday is the celebration of the birth of Christ Jesus, God's only son. The sad part is that many of the people celebrating

Jesus Christ's birthday do not have a personal relationship with the true living God or Jesus Christ. What are they really celebrating?

A True Confidant

I want you to picture being able to talk with a friend who never sleeps and is always ready to give you some wisdom. You share thoughts that no one else knows with this friend. You have the comfort in sharing what you fear with this friend. This friend loves you for who you are and not for selfish reasons. You can share your dreams and goals with this friend without being ridiculed or laughed at. This friend will motivate you with the truth and not with deception or embellishment. This true friend will not give you false hope, abandon you, or give up on you. This friend is dependable and reliable at all times. Now picture this friend as God. With God, everything is what it is. Nothing is hidden. God did not create us to live a life of confusion and loneliness. He doesn't want us wandering around and not knowing what to do with our lives.

Seeing People through God's Eyes

I love seeing people through God's eyes. No matter what age a person is or what he or she has done in life, God has purpose for him or her. When we see through God's eyes, we see the purpose of God in people and not everything they have done wrong in life.

Many people say, "God can use anybody who is open and willing to obey him."

There are times when God will move through an individual who doesn't meet the standard of the status quo. Some people will look for flaws to discredit others. We must not focus on the outward appearance of people because we will never see what God is seeing or doing in their lives. We all have issues that God wants to help us resolve so that we can have inner peace. I love the fact that God looks at the heart of people and not the outside. God is not impressed by our outer beauty, our intellect, our earthy possessions (cars, houses, clothes, degrees), or our bank accounts. God has a bigger plan for our lives.

I love the story in the Bible when God instructed Samuel to go to a man named Jesse. Jesse had many sons, and one of them was to be chosen as the king of Israel. When Jesse's son Eliab passed by Samuel, it seemed good to Samuel that he would be God's anointed. God told Samuel not to look on his countenance or his height. God told Samuel that people look at outward appearances, but God looks at people's hearts. Jesse allowed seven of his sons to pass before Samuel, but God did not choose any of them.

Samuel asked Jesse if he had any more sons, and Jesse called for his youngest son who was tending the sheep. When Samuel saw David's ruddy complexion and beautiful countenance, the Lord told Samuel to anoint him with oil.

We often respond to what we see on the outside of people without looking at their inner qualities. Some people say, "You don't look like the type to work, cook, sing, do artwork, or dance." I have had people ask me if I cook because apparently I don't look like I can cook. Some things are just funny when you think about them. I imagine David was thought of last because he was thought of as the least likely to be considered a king. God turned some heads when he anointed David.

I remember hearing several horrible stories about a woman. Even though I had heard bad things about her, I began to pray and see her as God saw her. I heard what God was saying about her. My heart was touched by the overflowing love and care that God has for her, and she didn't even know it. As I began to share the words of the Lord with her, she wept. It is vital that we see through the eyes of God so we can see people God's way and not in our own way.

Stop Trying to Understand Everything in Life

You may have noticed how people always want an explanation for everything that happens in life. When there is nothing to figure out or people can't wrap their brains around something, frustration sets in. Sometimes it is safe to say, "I don't know what is happening."

I have tried to explain why I do some things, but I realize that no one will ever understand me the way God does. He is the only one who will ever understand me to the fullest. I am so at ease with myself now. I don't expect people to fully understand me because they shouldn't have to—and they never will.

As a young mother, I was divorced. I had gone through some difficult times and was in need of a confidant and a true friend. I found the Lord to be an infinitely wise counselor, healer, consoler, defender, and compassionate friend. I've learned to rely and trust in him since he said, "For my thoughts are not your thoughts, neither are your ways, saith the Lord. For as the heavens are higher than the earth, so are my ways higher than your ways, and my thoughts than your thoughts" (Isaiah 55:8–9 AMP). The Lord will always be with me and will never leave me.

God Wants to Talk with You

I shared the following words with a young lady on August 25, 2011. I hope you find them helpful. Is God talking to you through your dreams? This is one of the many ways he will come in and speak to us and get our attention. You have questions, and God has all the answers. You are not certain of whether you hear him clearly when he is speaking or if you simply do not hear him when he is speaking to you. God will speak to you through dreams to get your attention. If you are uncertain of your purpose here on earth, then God can help you.

God does not want you to be uncertain or confused by this. God knew you before the foundations of the world, before you were even formed in your mother's womb. He has placed great gifts within you that will bring him glory. Yes, you were born with a defined destiny and purpose. God will reveal it to you when you seek him and draw unto him. Pray and ask him to show you. Pray and ask God to fill you with the Holy Spirit. He will guide you and lead you to the truth. Your desire should be to see yourself as God sees you. You were not born to walk around confused or feeling lost and in over your head.

God is revealing his thoughts about us as his creation. God is revealing his expectations for us to succeed in life. God is revealing to us that he is concerned about our cares and that he hears us and will answer us. He reveals how we will need him for vital necessity.

God spoke to Jeremiah about Israel, and he is still speaking this way to us today.

> For I know the thoughts and plans that I have for you, says the Lord, thoughts and plans for welfare and peace and not for evil, to give you hope in your final outcome. Then you will call upon Me, and you will come and pray to Me, and I will hear and heed you. Then you will seek Me, inquire for, and require Me (as a vital necessity) and find Me when you search for Me with all your heart. (Jeremiah 29:11–13)

God is always able to do abundantly above all that we can ask or think according to the power that works in us (Ephesians 3:20). This power, of course, is the Holy Spirit.

For Review

- Think of someone who has had a great impact on your life. What impact has he or she made on your life? Do you think it was because this person discovered his or her purpose and walked in it?
- Define the word *simplicity*. What does simplicity mean to God?
- Explain how we are able to see people through the eyes of God.
- What is God saying to you? Get a pad and pen. Find a quiet place and begin to talk with God. Bind up all outside voices (demonic influences) and selfish desires (what is contrary to the Spirit). Ask the Holy Spirit to minister the Father's love to you. Write down what you see or hear.
- Explain God's thoughts and plans for us in Jeremiah 29:11–13.

Chapter Four

The Mighty Warrior

The Lord is our mighty warrior, and he wins all of his battles. The scriptures refer to God as a mighty man who will stir up zealous indignation and vengeance. "The Lord will go forth like a mighty man; He will rouse up His zealous indignation and vengeance" (Isaiah 42:13).

When God desires to see a thing complete, he will choose one who will yield, submit, trust, obey, and labor with him in his kingdom business. Picture a strong king getting ready to go into battle with a determined mind-set to be victorious over his enemies. The wise king has appointed key people in specific positions to help win the battle and the war. These key people see the king's vision. They see the king being victorious, agree with the king, and want to accomplish the mission. God wants his righteous kingdom to operate on earth as it is in heaven.

People in the Bible Saw and Knew God as a Mighty Warrior

King David spoke about God's power.

> By the word of the Lord were the heavens made, and their entire host by the breath of His mouth. He gathers the waters of the sea as in a bottle; He puts the deeps in storage places. Let all the earth fear the Lord [revere and worship Him]; let all the inhabitants of the world stand in awe of Him. For He spoke and it was done; He commanded, and it stood fast. The Lord brings the counsel of the nations to naught; He makes the thoughts and plans of the peoples of no effect. The counsel of the Lord stands forever, the thoughts of His heart through all generations. (Psalm 33:6–11, AMP)

Let's look at Elijah and the prophets of Baal in 1 Kings 30:36–39. Elijah had great confidence in God. He knew what God was capable of doing, and Elijah prayed that all of Israel would know of the mighty God in Israel. Elijah and the prophets of Baal had prepared their offering of the evening sacrifice.

> Elijah the prophet came near and said, "O Lord, the God of Abraham, Isaac, and Israel, let it be known this day that you are God in Israel and that I am your servant and that I have done all these things at your word. Hear me, O Lord, hear me that this people may know that you, the Lord, are God, and have turned their hearts back to you." Then the fire of the Lord fell and consumed the burnt sacrifice and the wood and the stones and the dust, and also licked up the water that was in the trench. When all the people saw it, they fell on their faces and they said,

"The Lord, He is God! The Lord, He is God!" (1 Kings 18:36–39)

Jehu Defeats Jezebel

Jehu had great confidence in God and was obedient to the Word of God. Jehu at the leading of the Lord God defeated Jezebel at Jezreel, who ordered many of God's prophets to be killed (2 Kings 9:30–33).

When Jezebel heard that Jehu was coming to Jezreel, she painted her eyes, beautified her head, and looked out of an upper window. As Jehu entered the gate, she said, "Have you come in peace, you Zimri, who slew his master?"

Jehu lifted up his face to the window and said, "Who is on my side? Who?" When two or three eunuchs looked out at Jehu, he said, "Throw her down!"

They threw her down, and some of her blood splattered on the wall and on the horses, and he drove over her.

Caleb Fights for His Inheritance

Caleb was eighty-five years old when he declared that his strength and confidence in the Lord helped him fight for his inheritance.

> Yet I am as strong today as I was the day Moses sent me; as my strength was then, so is my strength now for war and to go out and to come in. So now give me this hill country of which the Lord spoke that day. For you heard then how the (giant like) Anakim were there and that the cities were great and fortified; if the Lord will be with me, I shall drive them out just as the Lord said. (Joshua 14:11–12)

Caleb knew God was a mighty warrior who was good on his promises. Therefore, Joshua blessed Caleb and gave him Hebron. With the Lord's help, Hebron became the inheritance of Caleb.

For Review

- Explain Caleb's attitude toward his inheritance promised to him by God.
- What is it about God that King David speaks on in Psalm 33:6–11?
- Study the examples. What are some of the key characteristics that each of these people had in common?

There Is No Limit to What God Can Do

Infinite Healer

There is no limit as to what God can heal. Jesus Christ paid the ultimate price for us. Jesus Christ has redeemed us back to God, and his blood has covered our sins. Jesus Christ has paved the way for each of us to have unlimited access to God. The blood of Jesus Christ makes us whole from every kind of illness. We no longer have to go to an earthy priest to confess our sins. We can confess our wrongdoing right before God, and he will forgive us. We can ask God to heal and restore us spiritually, physically, mentally, and emotionally—and he is able to do exactly that. We must be willing to pray in faith, believing God will perform it.

While working as a therapist's assistant in a nursing home and a hospital, I was surrounded by illness and hopeless people. The experience of serving the elderly changed my life. I enjoyed spending time and talking with the elderly. The Lord would lead me to certain individuals and had me pray with them. Some of them prayed to receive the Holy Spirit. Through prayer and faith, I have witnessed God healing and restoring a seventy-nine-year-old cancer patient. Through prayer and faith, I have witnessed God healing and restoring movement to a woman after a stroke.

I witnessed God healing and restoring an elderly woman with the strength to walk again after a fall at home left her swollen, stiff, and unable to move. After six weeks, she could move again, and her entire body was flexible. While working in the intensive care unit at the hospital, I would pray and sometimes sing over the patients if they were unresponsive. One particular patient was in a coma. As I was singing and performing passive range of motion to her arms, I saw her legs and feet swaying back and forth. I stared in awe at what was happening. Within a few weeks, the woman woke up and was responsive. This was wonderful news. There were many other healing stories to share, but the main point I'm making is that God is a mighty healer.

I've even seen God eliminate debt. The individual's real name has been replaced with Jane. Many years ago, someone stole Jane's checkbook and quickly wrote several bad checks in her name. The individual wrote many checks before Jane realized that her checkbook was missing. Jane notified her bank that she had nothing to do with the bad checks. Her account was put on hold so any other checks would not bounce, but she would have to deal with the debt. There were at least nine bad checks. The debt was overwhelming because of fees and other charges. She received letters demanding full payment and threats of being arrested if she didn't pay for the bad checks.

Jane prayed and asked the Lord for help. She paid off two bad checks and was proceeding to pay off a third one. After about three months, Jane made a phone call in an attempt to pay off another check. As she released information to the debt collector who would identify her case number, something remarkably strange happened. After several attempts to retrieve Jane's case number, the person found no record of Jane in the system. Jane wanted to be certain that it was all clear, and she had them search three times, but they didn't find anything. The person told her that there was nothing to pay. The person couldn't find any information on the checks Jane had actually paid.

For Review

- How awesome is it that Christ has paved the way for each of us to have unlimited access to God? What does this mean to you?
- What have you witnessed God healing and restoring in your life or someone else's life? How did it make you feel?
- Explain how the blood of Jesus Christ has paid the ultimate price for us.
- What is the significance of prayer and faith working together?

Chapter Five

How Do You See God?

We don't always have to use words to express our trust and faith in God. Our actions will reveal it all. Anybody can say, "I trust God in everything and all situations," but our actions will show and tell where we stand.

Anybody can quote a scripture—even a person who can't read can quote a scripture after hearing it—but the application of the words makes the difference. How one views God determines how one responds to God. Do you see God as nonexistent? If you see God as nonexistent, you will dismiss or disregard all the possibilities of him existing. Do you see God as being mean and distant? If you believe that God exists, but you see him as being mean and difficult to access, you will not bother to come to him. Who wants to have a relationship with a mean God who is difficult to access? Do you see God as being small and frail? If you believe in God, but see him as being a small, frail, and loving God who can only handle a few things at a time, you will only trust God with the things you think he is capable of handling.

Do you see God as being nice and think that he will agree to let you live any kind of way and do whatever you want without consequences? There is life in Christ Jesus that is of abundance, but this doesn't mean we are to live in any kind of way. God did not give his only son to die on the cross for the salvation of people because he was being nice. God did this because of his love for mankind.

If you think God can be manipulated or bought by flattery words and works, then this is exactly how you will approach God. God sees the true heart of people. He knows our intentions and motives before we even come to him. Christians can be viewed as nice because of kindness, meekness, and generosity toward people. This should not be seen as a weakness because they are simply demonstrating the fruits of the spirit.

Some unbelievers are kind and generous and give of themselves naturally to a certain level, but there is always room for improvement. God gives all true believers in Jesus his spirit so we can bear his fruits. The Word of God tells us that the fruit of the Holy Spirit is love, joy, peace, kindness, goodness, faith, gentleness, and self-control. Against such things, there is no law (Galatians 5:22–23).

According to the *Strong's Exhaustive Concordance,* the word *nice* is not in the Bible. According to the *Merriam-Webster's Dictionary, nice* was first used in English five hundred years ago to mean "foolish or stupid." It came through early French from the Latin *nescius,* meaning "ignorant." By the sixteenth century, the sense of being "very particular" or "finicky" had developed. In the nineteenth century, *nice* came to mean "pleasant or agreeable" and then "respectable," a sense quite unlike its original meaning. By 1913, *nice* was used to describe foolish, silly, simple, ignorant, weak, or effeminate (to make womanly, to unman, having behavior or mannerisms considered feminine or typical of a woman or girl).

I have had many people refer to me as a "nice" person. Many of them had hopes of taking advantage of me by asking me to do things that they would have never asked other individuals to do. And they would not have done these things for me or anyone else. They have spoken words of disrespect that they certainly would not have spoken to other individuals. They have tried to give me items that were suitable for the dumpster. They have shown me great partiality, deception, and manipulation while praising me for being nice. My kindness and generosity are sadly mistaken for being gullible and weak. When I didn't give in to their manipulative requests, I discovered that their perception of me changed.

Do you see God as gargantuan? God is tremendous in size and volume. God is strong, wise, sovereign, kindhearted, understanding, loving, gracious, merciful, generous, honest, trustworthy, loyal, unconquerable, and undefeatable. He has integrity and is forever present. He is always ready to assist anyone who will believe, trust, or call out to him.

God is not human; he is a spirit. God is not limited to time or the earthly elements as we are. He is not limited in knowledge or wisdom. For every brilliant person you can think of, I can name one who is more brilliant. You may have figured it out already. God is more brilliant than we are, and his thoughts surpass all of our understanding. God is a spirit, and those who worship him must worship him in spirit and in truth (John 4:24).

We can't buy a statue or some type of deity figure and call it God. We can't put on a performance of entertainment and hope to get God's approval. It is not by our works that we are granted salvation unto the Lord. It is by grace that we obtain salvation. We must be willing to come wholeheartedly to God. We must be willing to accept his son Jesus as our Lord and Savior. We must be willing to trust and obey God. If we don't trust God, it will be impossible for us to please him. God has given mankind biblical principles to live by that help us to be fruitful and not to live in depravity.

God's Kingdom Way Is the Better Way

There is a standard in the kingdom of God that is not of the world. When Christians mix and mingle humanism and socialism with God's kingdom's standards, we are operating in perversion. One of the tactics the enemy (Satan) uses to destroy people is to infiltrate them with perversion. Satan influences many people to distort and corrupt God's original kingdom's purpose for mankind. For example, some financial experts teach that college loans, car loans, and mortgages are considered good debt. Many people have bought into this deception and are now working extra hard to get out of debt. I have developed a budget to pay back my school loans in a shorter time than was scheduled.

Many people retire from jobs that are the main sources of income and get other jobs to create more cash flow, but they are still in debt. I hunger for the wisdom of God that will advance my family and me into a life of abundance.

Jesus said, "The thief (Satan) comes only in order to steal, kill, and destroy. I came that they may have and enjoy life and have it in abundance (to the full till it overflows)" (John 10:10, AMP).

Human Wisdom versus God's Wisdom

Many people rely on human wisdom instead of God's wisdom, and they don't get very far because it is nothing compared to godly wisdom. "Because the foolishness of God is wiser than men, and the weakness of God is stronger than men" (1 Corinthians 1:25).

"For this world's wisdom is foolishness (absurdity and stupidity) with God, for it is written, He lays hold of the wise in their (own) craftiness" (1 Corinthians 3:19, AMP).

Why are so many people in debt? Could it be because of greed and people relying on human wisdom to solve matters? It is very safe to say that the government relies more on human wisdom than on godly wisdom. That is why we have to pray and seek out honest godly men and women to appoint to the government. God did not intend for people to live from paycheck to paycheck. Debt is debt—no matter how you try to dress it up. Debt keeps you from enjoying life the way you would like to live—and the way that God intended for you to live. Debt restricts you from being a generous giver, and it can take away your joy.

Giving Creates Blessings

My husband and I both are generous givers, and we love to give. This doesn't mean that we give to everything. We always pray over what we invest in. We sow seeds into more than one ministry because we are givers. One time we were hit hard in our finances and weren't able to give as we wanted to. We became cranky and frustrated. We felt confined and restricted and had no room to breathe.

My husband had an idea to sell our few pieces of jewelry at a pawnshop. We were happy and thankful for the ninety dollars we got in exchange for the pieces of jewelry. We then gave the ninety dollars as an offering. We have witnessed tremendous blessings from applying godly wisdom. Know that giving is not limited to money. Giving can be time, gifts, skills, kind words, or items. Giving is a two-way channel—not a one-way channel. When we give and bless others, God will bless us. I firmly believe that God has given us multiple ways of creating wealth or income for provision. When you are blessed, you are able to be a blessing to others.

This is why it is necessary for true believers of Jesus to first seek the kingdom of God and his righteousness so that all our basic needs will be given to us (Matthew 6:33). To seek means to aim toward and strive after something. In following God, we should aim and strive to know his way of being kingdom-minded and living from a kingdom perspective. We are able to do this because the kingdom of God is within us (Luke 17:21).

The kingdom of God is in the heart of every true born-again believer. The kingdom is of righteousness, peace, and joy in the Holy Spirit (Romans 14:17). Everyone who serves Christ in this manner is acceptable and pleasing to God and is approved by men (Romans 14:18). It does not say the kingdom is of hopelessness, bondage, depravity, debt, depression, shame, or poverty. How many people do you know are happy and overtaken by joy in their lives because they are living in God's way (the kingdom way)?

For Review

- Explain what it means to come wholeheartedly to God.
- Who do you see God as in your life? Be specific.
- We see that the fruit of the Holy Spirit is love, joy, peace, kindness, goodness, faith, gentleness, and self-control. Do a self-evaluation. Be honest. Do you have the fruit of the Holy Spirit operating in your life? Always pray and ask the Holy Spirit to help you with your weaknesses.
- Which of the fruits of the Holy Spirit are your strongest?
- Which of the fruits of the Holy Spirit are your weakest?

- Do you only trust God in the things that you think he is capable of handling?
- What is the difference between godly wisdom and human wisdom? If you are a Christian, examine your thoughts and actions. Which of the two do you tend to lean toward?

Chapter Six

God's Infinite Thoughts toward His People

One day while worshipping in an assembly among other saints, the presence of God was very prevalent. As we continued to worship, angelic activity came into the building. People began to receive individual personal letters from the angels. I saw the words "I love you" in bold print before my face. The words were there for only a few seconds before they vanished. I wept so deeply and quietly. I told God that I loved him too. Many others began to speak of what they had seen in their angelic letters. Everyone was rejoicing.

Before this heart-touching surprise, I told God almost every day how much I loved him. I would tell him while cooking, cleaning, doing schoolwork, watching TV, and taking a shower. I really enjoyed telling God that I love him. Later that day, I was journaling about what had happened during the service. While I was writing the words "I love you," I began to hear some of the names of God and what each name meant. I began to break down the words "I love you." As I continued to write, I could sense how much compassion and love God has for me, his creation.

I

The Lord God Almighty is the Alpha and Omega, the beginning and the end. I am that I am.

- *Jehovah El Shaddai*—the all-sufficient One, the God who is more than enough, the almighty God
- *Jehovah Shalom*—the Lord is my peace
- *Jehovah Roha*—my shepherd
- *Elohim*—the God who creates
- *Jehovah Jirah*—my provider
- *Jehovah Mescadesh*—the God who sanctified
- *Jehovah Shamah*—the presence of the Lord
- *Jehovah Nissi*—the Lord is my banner and conqueror
- *Jehovah Elyon*—the Lord God most high
- *Jehovah Sabaoth*—the Lord of Hosts is a warrior, the Lord of armies
- *Jehovah Tsidkenu*—the Lord is our righteousness
- *Jehovah Repheka*—the Lord is my healer

Love

The excellence of love is patience. Love is kind and is not jealous. Love does not brag and is not arrogant. Love does not act unbecomingly or seek its own. Love is not provoked. It does not take into account a wrong suffered. It does not rejoice in unrighteousness, but it rejoices with the truth. Love bears all things and endures all things. Love never fails (1 Corinthians 13:4).

God demonstrated his own love toward us. While we were still sinners, Christ died for us (Romans 5:8).

You

I am his masterpiece for purpose (Ephesians 2:10). He chose me before the foundation of the world (Ephesians 1:4). Intimately loved and chosen by God, he knitted me together in my mother's womb and brought me forth to life at the right, precise time. He has given me unique abilities to do things that no one else can do to fulfill my God-given assignment on earth.

> My frame was not hidden from You (God) when I was being formed in secret (and) intricately and curiously wrought (as if embroidered with various colors) in the depths of the earth (a region of darkness and mystery). Your eyes saw my unformed substance, and in your book all the days (of my life) were written before ever they took shape, when as yet there was none of them (Psalm 139:15, 16 AMP).

"How precious and weighty also are your thoughts to me, O God! How vast is the sum of them! If I could count them, they would be more in number than the sand" (Psalm 139:17, 18 AMP).

God speaks of how he knows his own thoughts and plans that he has for us (Jeremiah 29:11). His thoughts and plans are for our well-being and peace. God's thoughts toward us are not evil. His thoughts are good and give us hope in our expected ends. The Creator had pure significant thoughts toward his creations from the beginning of mankind. There is nothing I had to do for God's love. It has been there from the beginning because God is love.

For Review

- The names of God reveal something about him. Meditate over the names of God and their meanings. Think about Jehovah El Shaddai—the all-sufficient One—the God who is more than enough. Describe what this means to you.
- Explain what being God's masterpiece for a purpose means.
- What has God given you that will help you fulfill your God-given assignment on earth?
- We know that God's thoughts are good and that he thinks no evil toward us. Where do our negative thoughts come from?
- Romans 5:8 says, "God demonstrated His own love toward us, in that while we were yet sinners, Christ died for us." Explain what this means.
- Will a person's sins keep God from loving him or her?
- Will a person's sins keep God's presence away?

Chapter Seven

Our Obedience to the Mighty Warrior Gives Us Victory

God's obedient children will always have victory. The Lord began ministering to me on obedience on July 24, 2011. God requires obedience over sacrifice. When God gives us a command, we should want to do it—regardless of how we feel or think about it. We are to obey him because he is the Sovereign God. He is the God we confess that we believe in, trust, and love. When we disobey him, it is the same as doubt, disrespect, dishonor, and disregard for him. We are undermining him if we think God doesn't know what he is doing.

Who dares to bribe a king? When we offer a sacrifice to God while we are in disobedience, he doesn't want it—and he won't accept it. It is like attempting to bribe God; flattery words, works, and gifts can't buy him off. It's like offering God some garbage that belongs in the trash. This type of offering stinks with a foul order in his nostrils. After all, he is the Creator. He is the giver of all life.

What could people possible impart more than God? The answer is nothing. What sense would it make to give an offering to God if you doubt, distrust, disrespect, or dishonor him?

The Lord makes it very clear of where he stands when it comes to obedience over sacrifice. We will look at Saul, the king of Israel. Saul's disobedience to God's command was attributed to his fear of people. King Saul waited seven days; according to the scheduled time he had appointed to come (1 Samuel 13:8–12). But Samuel had not come to Gilgal, and the people began to scatter from Saul in fear. King Saul took it upon himself to perform the burnt offering and the peace offerings, which he was forbidden to do.

God commanded Saul to destroy all the Amalekites and everything from Havilah (1 Samuel 15). He was told not to spare any of them, including the animals, but Saul did not obey the Lord. Saul justified his actions when Samuel questioned him. Samuel told Saul that he was rejected as king because he had rejected the Lord's Word. Saul admitted that his disobedience to the Lord was because he feared the people.

Saul revered the people more than God. He cared more about what the people thought than what God thought and he lost his place as king because of this. When we seek to please people out of fear, we always compromise the truth. When we fear people, we always act on our emotions and feelings. This will always result in doing something ridiculous with great consequences.

Every time I act out of fear of people to do something that seemed good or right, it brought on a dreadful, unwanted consequence. If you have ever allowed your feelings and emotions to guide you in a decision, I'm sure you understand where I'm coming from. Many people suffer from the fear of people, but they will not admit it. To truly have joy and be fruitful in life, one must be delivered from the fear of what people think and fear only the Lord. This does not mean that we disrespect or disobey authority figures. We are to obey authorities as long as it does not violate the commands of God. If a person is not completely faithful to what the Lord commands, there will be a continuation of disobedient actions. There will always be a price to pay for disobedience, and there will always be victory with obedience to the Lord. I pray to always be obedient to God.

For Review

- What did Saul do that was disobedient to the Lord?
- What was Saul's reason for not obeying the command of the Lord?
- What does the Bible have to say about rebellion? Why is God so against it?
- Take a few minutes to examine your life and see if you are compromising the Word of God in any area of your life. If so, what do you credit it to? What do you think will be your next action?

Chapter Eight

The Splendor of God

What God is as great as our God? You are the God who performs miracles; you display your power among the people (Psalm 77:14).

David speaks about how he will meditate on the glorious splendor of his majesty and on his wondrous works (Psalm 145:5). The splendor of God is always displayed through the acts of God. His splendor goes forth as he performs miraculous signs and wonders throughout the land.

This is also visible when the Lord brought Israel out of Egypt. The Lord used Moses and Aaron to deal with Pharaoh. "Moses told the people, Fear not; stand still (firm, confident, undismayed) and see the salvation of the Lord which He will work for you today. For the Egyptians you have seen today you shall never see again. The Lord will fight for you and you shall hold your peace and remain at rest" (Exodus 14:13–14, AMP).

"Israel saw that great work which the Lord did against the Egyptians, and the people [reverently] feared the Lord and trusted in (relied on, remained steadfast to) the Lord and to His servant Moses" (Exodus 14:31, AMP). "The Lord is a man of war; the Lord is His name" (Exodus 15:3).

This is visible in the story of Joshua defeating Amalek, a descendant of Esau (Exodus 17:8–13). Moses told Joshua to choose some men to fight with Amalek. Moses, Aaron, and Hur went to the top of a mountain. When Moses held up his hand with the rod of God, Israel prevailed. When he lowered his hand, Amalek prevailed. When his hands started to get heavy and grew weary, Aaron and Hur brought a stone for Moses to sit on.

Aaron and Hur held up his hands, one on each side, and his hands were supported. This enabled Joshua to prevail over Amalek and his people with the sword. Moses built an altar and said, "The Lord is my banner" (Exodus 17:15, AMP).

Jethro (Moses's father-in-law) said, "Blessed be the Lord, who has delivered you out of the hand of the Egyptians and out of the hand of Pharaoh, and who has delivered the people (Israel) from under the hand of the Egyptians. I know that the Lord is greater than all gods. Yes, in the (very) thing in which they dealt proudly (he showed himself infinitely superior to all their gods)" (Exodus 18:10–11, AMP). The Egyptians boast about their gods, but their many gods could not help them defeat Israel.

For Review

- Do you believe God performs miracles today? If so, can you picture God moving through in signs, miracles, and wonders to glorify him?
- How would you describe God's splendor?
- Describe the last time you beheld God's splendor. How did you respond to it?

- How has the Lord fought for you? Did you hold your peace and remain at rest?
- When Moses held up his hand with the rod of God, Israel prevailed, but when he lowered his hand, Amalek prevailed. When his hands started to grow weary, Aaron and Hur held up his hands. What do you suppose is the significance of this? Can you relate to this?

Chapter Nine

Trust in the Invincible God— No Matter What Happens

When we believe and come into agreement with God, we must be in total obedience with whatever God has for our destiny. All things that are of the Lord are possible with the invincible God. We must stay encouraged and go forth in God—no matter what happens.

While living in Colorado Springs, my son was accepted into a free public preschool program for low-income families. I was thankful for this, and my son enjoyed the classes. The bus would pick him up in the morning, but I was responsible for picking him up in the afternoon. I had a difficult time leaving work in time to pick up my son. I was a single mom with a part-time job as a physical therapist assistant, and I was in college. Almost every other day, I had to call someone to pick up my son. I was so thankful to have family and friends who could help me.

The Adventurous Challenges

My son began having a difficult time with learning in kindergarten and in second grade. We were living in El Paso, Texas, when the Lord began to drop it in my spirit to work with my son at home. I thought I was inadequate to teach him. Since I had a great fear of not teaching him the right way, I quickly enrolled him into a Christian academy school that exceeded our income. After giving our tithes and paying the regular bills, we simply had no room to breathe. It was not the right move for my son because he was still having difficulty learning. I finally came to my senses and surrendered to what the Lord had dropped in my spirit the first time about working with my son at home. The Lord awakened me one morning at two o'clock and had me research homeschooling.

As I began to read and understand more about it, I wondered whether I could do it. The Lord was encouraging me all the way through the transition. I heard a lot of questions about why I removed my son from public or private onsite campus dwellings. I explained that it was the leading of the Lord, and it was what my son needed. I had to make a decision. I could listen to people or trust and obey the Lord.

I made the decision to obey the Lord rather than the people around me who were asking me to reconsider my decision. The Lord guided me to the right curriculum for my son. When all was said and done, I was still nervous and clueless, but a burden had been released from me. From then on, I was excited and nervous. It would be a journey and an adventure for all of us. The good thing about the whole transition was that there was nothing to rush into because we were on a different schedule and had more time to sort out the technicalities. I enjoy learning new concepts when I don't have to rush through the material. Learning new things can be exciting and overwhelming at times, but with patience we gain new insight. My heart goes out to kids, teachers, and college students because of the extreme pressure that is demanded by education departments in many states.

Taken by Surprise

When we got the hang of the curriculum and found a schedule that worked for both of us, my son and I began to enjoy the flexibility and liberty of having school at home. The Lord even gave me other strategies to help my son learn. With diligent work, my son started doing well in all of his subject areas. Since he's not too fond of math or English, I tell him that they are his favorites.

As my daughter got older, I began teaching her as well. Homeschooling was far less stressful than the public schools. It was a great relief to not have my child bringing home a shopping list from school or papers that needed to be filled out, signed, and returned immediately. I don't miss this at all.

I would like to clarify some erroneous thoughts about children who are homeschooled. Just because they do their learning at home does not mean they are limited in their educations or learning capacities. It does not mean that their field trips are limited to the grocery store. It does not mean that they are deprived of social skills or restricted from extracurricular activities or sports. For example, my son has been playing drums and taking karate lessons on a weekly basis. He was on a basketball team for two years and attended a Christian summer camp while being homeschooled. On some weekends, he plays football or basketball with the other kids in the neighborhood. My daughter has been active in ballet and has taken weekly tap dance lessons; she also enjoys the outdoors.

God Can Make You Laugh Even When He Is Serious

While homeschooling my son, the Lord told me to go back to school to complete my bachelor's degree in health care. I did after he wouldn't accept my excuses. I told the Lord that going back to school would be too much for me while teaching my son and raising my daughter. I told the Lord that I would rather go to bible college and study the Word of God, but the Lord didn't respond for a little while. While I was sitting on my bed, I asked him about college.

He said, "You want to wait for when you think it's the right time, but now is the time to go. You are at home and can set your own schedule."

The Lord reminded me how I didn't have to get up early to drive the children to school or get up and drive to work. I thanked God for all the encouraging words and his infinite wisdom because it was true. I did as the Lord asked, and he eliminated any unnecessary classes on my behalf. This allowed me to take only the main classes for my degree. The Lord remembered my desire to study the Word of God, and he allowed me to receive a scholarship for Wagner Leadership Institute's School of Ministry. I was able to complete the classes at my very own pace while at home. Being obedient to God, I achieved my bachelor's degree in health care management within one year. Shortly thereafter, I received my bachelor's degree in practical ministry. After completing both degrees, the Lord instructed me to go for my master's degree in early childhood education.

In 2006, we were still living in El Paso, and my husband was deployed. Our daughter was five months old. For some reason, I felt compelled to take a program on child day care management. I actually enjoyed the program, but I didn't quite understand why I was taking it. I told God I didn't want to own a day care business because it was a lot of work.

One day, the Lord said, "I will use it."

I applied to the master's of education program. It would be another opportunity for God to affirm his provision and direction for my future. The time came for me to apply for the master's program in the education department.

They asked what teaching experience I had and what qualifications and certifications I held. Two prerequisite classes were mandatory since I didn't hold a bachelor's degree in childhood education.

I sat at my computer and asked, "Lord, what do I say?"

A few days later, I knew what to say. The Lord would use the four years of homeschooling the kids as hands-on training. I submitted my application, and I had an answer within four days. To my surprise, I was accepted into the program, and three classes were waived on my behalf. Two of the waived classes were the mandatory prerequisite classes. I only had to complete nine classes instead of twelve. To affirm his approval even the more, the Lord had a young preschool teacher give me an abundance of preschool resources and supplies that would carry me through the final major classes in the program. I would even use the majority of the resources in teaching my daughter.

Great Things Are Possible with the Invincible God

In the midst of going back to school and homeschooling my son and daughter, the Lord placed it on our hearts in 2010 to open our home as a haven. I thought *this is a lot*. Then I remembered that the

Lord's grace would carry us through whatever he asked us to do. We needed to trust him.

Our home became a place where we would minister to the weak and wounded and speak life into them. There were only a few of us, and we didn't mind it at all. We were so excited about what would happen in the midst of us. We wondered what God was going to do the next time we met. We wanted the presence of God and not just a house full of people. Some people are only after the quantities in God, and some are after the qualities in God. Life is not about how much I can get from God to prove that he is with me. Life is allowing God to live and reveal himself through us so that God's kingdom will operate on the earth.

How did we get the name Haven? We prayed and asked God to give us a creative, unique name that would describe the ministry work in our home. My husband and I had witnessed the Lord doing so many great things in our lives and touching the lives of others through our obedience to him. I was obedient when God told me to go back to school, and within a year and a half, I received my master's degree in early childhood education. This was in total agreement with God all the way. Yes, Lord!

Recognizing an Opportunity of the Lord

After about a year of ministering in our home, we then received orders to PCS (permanent change of station) to another duty station. Our new location would be Honolulu (Fort Shafter). This would make my second trip to Hawaii in seventeen years. I had always hoped to revisit the beautiful island. Who would have known but the Lord that I would one day be returning with my family? Although living in Hawaii sounds awesome—and we were thankful for getting the orders—it would be another exciting, adventurous, challenging assignment for us. Hawaii is a beautiful place to visit; for many, it is a place to call home. That didn't mean that there were no obstacles or oppositions. We decided to trust the invincible God—no matter what happened.

Recognizing the Good Things

My son was so excited about living in Hawaii, and he asked if he could try to attend school there. My husband was fond of the idea, but I had reservations about the whole matter. I was concerned about my son being focused enough to complete his work and dealing with peer pressure as a young boy, but I figured it wouldn't hurt to try. After consulting with the Lord on the matter, we agreed to give it a shot.

At the first teacher-parent meeting, the teacher spoke about how respectful and well behaved our son was toward her and the other students. The teacher told us how well he was getting along with other students. She told us which subject areas he struggled in, how he was very distracted by other classmates, and how he wouldn't complete some of his assignments on time. We already knew this and were not a bit surprised. My husband and I were pleased to hear how well he conducted himself and how he was adjusting to the new learning environment. I was delighted to see his handwritten paragraphs with five complete sentences. I was actually impressed by how far he had progressed in his reading skills.

Several weeks later, I was asked to attend another meeting about our son. She suggested that we have our son screened and tested for multiple learning deficits. Some sort of prescription might help him focus. All we had to do was sign some papers and return them to school, but after consulting with the Lord, we did not agree with this option. Instead, we agreed to continue homeschooling our son with Christian workbooks in all five subjects.

My son frequently reminds me about what he likes with homeschooling. While spending some quiet time alone, I thought about when I was eight years old. I always wanted to play school with my younger siblings and cousins. I would be the teacher, and the smaller kids would be the students. I even talked to one of my friends from high school about wanting to home school my children one day. All I could do was smile at how I had forgotten those words.

I am still homeschooling my kids, and I enjoy spending quality time with them. Of course, it can be challenging at times, but this is expected.

Prayer Gives Direction and Guidance

One of the things my husband and I spent a lot of time doing when we first arrived to Hawaii was intercession. We spent a lot of time praying about his job position and location. We spent hours in prayer over the region and asking the Lord for directions. We would do our part and watch God do what we couldn't do, which was the impossible.

While living at Fort Shafter Flats, we began a prayer and study session at a local middle school. We would intercede for all the schools on the island and on the mainland. Many times, it would only be our family and a few other individuals. We would pray for them as they would come and speak about their lives. The Lord let it be known that he was listening and watching our attitudes in each gathering.

Lead the Children to Christ

We opened our home to the children in our neighborhood and taught them about God, Jesus, and biblical principles to live by. My husband and I would go out and talk to some of the parents. We wanted to build a rapport with the parents, and we did with some. The good thing about it was that the kids actually wanted to come hear about God, but we had to really pray that the parents would let the kids come into our home.

My son and daughter would go out early and gather kids who wanted to come—and who had permission from their parents. Some parents would let their kid come late or require the kid to come home early. Some wouldn't let their kids come until it was completely over. The children would dance, pray for one another, rap, and sing songs. We made crafts and treated the kids to bowling or a movie. The children had many questions about God, Jesus, and heaven, and we did our best to teach them. It was a battle worth fighting for, but it wasn't a long battle.

Embracing the Shifting

The things that the Lord asks you to do are not always permanent. You won't be doing them forever. Sometimes the Lord asks you to do something for a season. Sometimes, the Lord is testing you and preparing you for something even greater.

Toward the end of 2012, we began experiencing a shifting in the Holy Spirit and felt change around us. We knew that the Lord was bringing something to an end. We didn't know the reason for it, but we could certainly feel the internal shift. And then we began to see it externally, all around us.

It isn't always easy to embrace change. Sometimes we get attached and feel comfortable with what we are doing. We feel we have everything under control because we have confidence that we know what to do. When the Lord puts something to do on your heart—and you actually look forward to it and enjoy doing it—you will need to accept the ending and embrace the beginning of something new. Of course this doesn't mean you won't shed any tears. It is all right if you do or if you don't. Sometimes you celebrate within because you are grateful that he has brought something to an end.

When my husband was shifted into a new brigade on another post, the intercession and cell group were shifted to our home. The Sunday gatherings with the kids came to a close. Whether it was one kid or five kids, we gave our best to glorify God. I cried many nights because I really missed teaching the kids about Jesus. You can't explain something to kids—or adults—that you don't understand. The only thing to do is trust God through the shifting.

On certain occasions, we have the kids over, and they enjoy themselves as usual. We really enjoy giving to the children and sharing the love of God. The Lord loves children and greatly desires for them to know the truth about him.

Embracing a New Assignment

On December 31, 2012, the Lord gave me the birthing for IFOC (Interceding for Our Children), and my heart beats passionately for it. We know that there is a dark, evil force in operation against the unborn child and all children across the world. This violent murdering spirit has swept across our nation for too many years. When people have a heart and passion to save and protect animals, animal eggs, various species of creatures, trees, and rainforests, but could care less about protecting the life of their own mankind, it is a serious problem. We have laws set in place to protect animals from abuse and neglect of caregivers and owners, but no strict laws protect the innocent unborn child. It is a good thing to protect animals from abuse, but by all means, the same should be implemented for the life of a helpless, fragile unborn child.

This same demonic force is attacking our schools. There is a war going on against our innocent children. I go into more detail about it at the back of the book.

Prayer Prepares You for What Is Ahead

Trust in the invincible God—no matter what happens. Things will not always go as planned. Therefore, you must be willing to press forward—no matter how things look from the outside. In the midst of homeschooling the kids, working diligently at finishing this book, and launching my nonprofit organization, my husband received orders for deployment. We prayed and asked God not to have him go. It wasn't that we didn't trust God to protect him from harm; it was because we were a team and had many exciting things that we were looking forward to doing together as a family. We had planned to visit another island since we were already in Hawaii. We had to postpone the trip. We prayed and we prayed. God would share words of encouragement with us as we prayed. All of our praying was really preparing our family for what was ahead.

On Sunday September 28, 2013, my husband was deployed to Afghanistan with an engineer brigade. This was very unpleasant for our family because we didn't want Jermaine to leave. We double-checked the manifest to make sure his name was not on the list. Since God had removed his name from the manifest once before, sparing him from deployment, we asked God to do it again. It would be my husband's fourth deployment.

In spite of what we were asking God to do, he had a greater plan that was far ahead of us. This deployment would be different from all the other deployments. The Lord assured my husband and me that he would be away for only a short time and then return home stronger in God than when he left. The Lord gave my kids and me an inner peace that passes all understanding. Our entire family has faithful intercessors covering us with prayer. Feeling the prayers on our behalf brought great tranquility to our family. I expect to see and hear the numerous testimonies that will flow from him like a river.

In December 2013, my husband left Afghanistan with the other soldiers and returned to Hawaii. He was scheduled to be deployed in Afghanistan for nine months. Instead of nine months, it would be two months. In the meantime, we patiently awaited his return. I focused on teaching our kids and perusing the assignments God has instructed for me to do and for us to do as a family. On December 12, 2013 my husband returned home. The invincible God is always faithful to his promises.

Chapter Ten

Access to the Invincible God through Christ Jesus

We all have access to the invincible God through Christ Jesus.

In John 1:1, God's son is being introduced as the Word (Logos). Jesus is the essence of God's revelation. Jesus is referred to as the Lamb of God because he provides salvation for whoever believes in (trusts in, adheres to, relies on) him. The words in parentheses occur ninety-eight times throughout John's gospel. All who believe and have faith in Jesus Christ are assured the possession of eternal life with him.

God's signs and wonders are evidence of his supernatural power in areas of life where mankind is impotent.

> Whosoever believes that Jesus is the Christ, the Son of God and that through believing he might obtain eternal life. God so greatly loved and dearly prized the world

> that He (even) gave up His only begotten (unique) Son, so that whoever believes in (trusts in, clings to, relies on) Him shall not perish (come to destruction, be lost) but have eternal (everlasting) life. God did not send the Son into the world in order to judge (to reject, to condemn, to pass sentence on) the world, but that the world might find salvation and be made safe and sound through Him. (John 3:16–17)

Accept the Lord Jesus Christ into your heart as your personal Savior and repent (acknowledge, confess wrongdoings, and turn away from them).

"That if thou shalt confess with thy mouth the Lord Jesus, and shalt believe in thine heart that God hath raised Him from the dead, thou shalt be saved" (Romans 10:9).

Below is a simple prayer for anyone and everyone who would desire to be a son or daughter of the Most High God. God showed himself to be invincible through Christ Jesus when he conquered the grave and through the healings that Jesus performed.

> Lord Jesus, I believe that you are the Son of God and that you died for me and rose up on the third day with all power in your hands. I confess I am a sinner (one who sins against God's Word). I ask you to forgive my sins and come into my heart. I receive your love, peace, and eternal life with you, Lord. I ask you to affirm your love by giving me bountiful peace, joy, and love for all people.

Pray and ask God to fill you with the Holy Spirit, and he will guide and lead you in all truth. When you have confessed this and truly mean it, you are his. Don't let the enemy (devil) or anyone else tell you anything different. You can confess this daily. You belong to the Lord. His desire is for you to know him and have a personal relationship with him.

When we give our lives to the Lord, we are giving him permission to deliver us and save us from destruction and death. We must be willing to surrender and yield our willpower (what we want, how we want, how we want to live, and everything that feeds our flesh) to God.

In Closing

I hope this book has helped you experience the invincible God's power, grace, compassion, patience, mercy, and loving kindness. God is good to his creations. His deepest desire is for mankind to know him as the invincible God and to trust in him. His loving kindness is far greater than any earthly materials we can possess. I pray that you desire to draw closer and develop a deeper, more intimate relationship with God. I pray that it will inspire you to have an unquenchable hunger for the Word of God and that you will not go another day without seeing God as unconquerable and undefeatable.

Personal Testimonies of God Ministering through Me in Prophetic Songs

Moving All over the Land

In February 2009, I was sitting at my desktop computer and working on a school paper. I decided to check the news and began to read about what was going on with the economy. There was much talk about the stock market, the housing crises, businesses going broke and closing, and high unemployment rates.

I began to hear words and a tune in my spirit. For days, I sang the song around my house day and night. Within a couple of weeks, the Lord gave me another verse to add to the song.

> I'm moving, I'm moving, I'm moving all over this land,
> Alpha, Omega, beginning and the end.
> Holy, righteous, mighty king,
> I'm moving, I'm moving, I'm moving all over this land.
> I'm moving, I'm moving, I'm moving all over this land.
> "Not by might, nor by power, but by my spirit," says
>   the Lord.
> "Not by might, nor by power, but by my spirit," says
>   the Lord.
> I'm moving, I'm moving, I'm moving all over this land.
> I'm moving, I'm moving, I'm moving all over this land.
> (Repeat)

Invincible God

In the beginning of March 2009, the Lord gave me the words to "Invincible God," and I sang this song around my home and with my children.

>You're an invincible God.
>You're an invincible God.
>You're unconquerable and undefeatable.
>You're unconquerable and undefeatable—invincible God.
>You're mighty, God. You're mighty, God.
>You're unconquerable, and undefeatable.
>You're unconquerable and undefeatable—invincible God.
>You win all battles. You win all battles.
>You're unconquerable and undefeatable—invincible God.
>You're an invincible God.
>You're an invincible God.
>You're unconquerable and undefeatable.
>You're unconquerable and undefeatable—invincible God.
>(Repeat)

Do It Again, God

>Do it again, God. Do it again.
>Do it again, God. Do it again.
>Let your power and demonstrations move throughout the land.
>Let the testimonies come forth. Let the testimonies arise.
>Move by your spirit, and show forth your splendor.
>Move, mighty warrior. Move, mighty God,
>invincible, unconquerable, undefeatable God.
>So do it again, God. Do it again. Do it again, God. Do it again.
>(Repeat)

Creation Worship Him—The Lord God Almighty

On March 15, 2009, at 4:50 a.m., I was awakened by an evil presence. I began to pray to the Holy Spirit and called upon the Lord.

The demon was determined to stay put.

I said, "In the name of Jesus, the Lord God rebukes you, and I command you to get out of this house and go to dry places."

I thought the demon would leave, but to my surprise, the evil presence didn't budge.

I asked the Lord what to do, and as he said, "Create an atmosphere of worship," I started thinking of a song to sing. The Lord gave me the words to "Where the Spirit of the Lord Is There Is Liberty." When I finished singing, he gave me a whole new song in my spirit. I could hear the tune, and the words began to flow from the Holy Spirit.

As I sang the words repeatedly, the atmosphere changed dramatically. When I realized the evil presence was gone, I continued to sing until I fell asleep.

When morning came, I couldn't wait to share the story with my husband when he called to check on us. He was in Columbia, South Carolina, for military training when this happened.

Creation Worship Him

The stars give a sound that makes music in his ears.
The sun and the moon proclaim his name.
The mountain and the rocks bow down to him.
Creation worships him.
Creation worships him.
Creation worships him.
Creation worships him, the Lord God Almighty.

The stars give a sound that makes music in his ears.
The sun and the moon proclaim his name.
The mountain and the rocks bow down to him.
Creation worships him.
(Repeat)

I Want to Be Free

I want to be free.
Free as I can be. Free as I can be.
I don't want to be lost. I don't want to be lost.
Free from all the doubt. Free from all the fears.
Free from everything that could hinder me.
I want to be free.
I want to be free.
Free as I can be. Free as God made me.
I don't want to be lost. I don't want to be lost.
I want to be free. Free from loneliness. Free from rejection.
Free from everything that could hinder me.
I want to be free. Free from peer pressure. Free from intimidation.
I don't want to be lost. I don't want to be lost.
I want to be free. Free from envy. Free from jealousy.
Free from everything that could hinder me.
I want to be free.
Free as I can be. Free as I can be.
Free from everything that could hinder me.
(Repeat)

Jesus Is Lord

There is a name above all names.
There is a name above all names.
There is a name above all names.
That every knee shall bow and every tongue confess,
Jesus is Lord. Jesus is Lord.
There is a name above all names.
There is a name above all names.
There is a name above all names.
That every knee shall bow and every tongue confess,
That Jesus reigns. That Jesus reigns.
That he is Lord. That he is Lord.
There is a name above all names.
That every knee shall bow and every tongue confess,
Jesus is Lord—Jesus is Lord.
(Repeat)

I'm Sold Out

We're living in a world where we can't make it without prayer.
We're living in a world where we can't make it by ourselves.
We need a Savior. We need a Deliverer.
And Jesus Christ was the ultimate sacrifice.
I don't know about you, but I've made my decision.
I've given my life to Christ, and I'm living for the true God.
I'm sold out. I'm sold out. I'm sold out. I'm sold out. I'm sold out. I'm sold out.
I'm sold out—to the living God.
(Repeat)

Open Heaven

There is an open heaven over me.
There is an open heaven over me.
And I can see—And I can hear
the Lord my God talking to me.
He is saying, "Run, run, my daughter, run."
He is saying, "Run, run, my daughter, run."
He is saying, "Run, run, my daughter, run,"
run with the vision I've given to you.
There is an open heaven over me.
There is an open heaven over me.
And I can see—And I can hear
the Lord my God talking to me.
I see the heavenly host backing me, and
he is saying, "Run, run, my daughter, run."
He is saying, "Run, run, my daughter, run."
He is saying, "Run, run, my daughter, run,
run with the vision I've given to you,"
repeating of words.

Only Want to Worship You

I only want to worship you.
I only want to worship you.
I only want to worship you, God,
for you are worthy of all the praise.
You are a righteous God.
You are a holy God.
You are a loving God,
for you are of all the praise.
I only want to worship you.
I only want to worship you.

I only want to worship to you God,
for you are worthy of all the praise.
You are a holy God.
You are a mighty God.
You are a Sovereign God,
for you are worthy of all the praise,
repeating of words.

There Is No Lacking in Jesus

There is no lacking in Jesus,
no lacking in Jesus.
He redeemed my soul.
He made me whole.
And now I rest in him.
There is no lacking in Jesus,
no lacking in Jesus.
He redeemed my soul.
He made me whole.
And now I rest in him.
(Repeat)

Recommended Reading

Hearing God, Spiritual Gifts, Spiritual Seasons, Discovering Dreams, and Purpose

> Murdock, Mike. *7 Signposts to Your Assignment*. Fort Worth, TX: The Wisdom Center, 2007.
> Pierce, D. Chuck., and Rebecca Wagner Sytsema. *When God Speaks*. Ventura, CA: Regal Books, 2005.
> Sheets, Dutch. *Dream: Discovering God's Purpose for Your Life*. Bloomington, MN: Bethany House Publishers, 2012.
> Swan, David. *Understanding the Spiritual Seasons of Life*. West Malaysia: Tabernacle of David, 2002.

The Apostolic

> Hagin, E. Kenneth. *The Believer's Authority*. Tulsa, Oklahoma: Kenneth Hagin Ministries, 2004.
> Swan, David. *The Davidic Generation: Understanding This Present Move of the Spirit*. West Malaysia: Tabernacle of David, 2005.
> Swan, David. *Passion for the Glory*. Tabernacle of David, 2006.

The Prophetic

David, Dr. Jonathan. *Moving in the Gifts of Revelation and Prophecy.* Johor, Malaysia: Full Gospel Centre Muar, 2007.

Deere, Jack. *The Beginner's Guide to the Gift of Prophecy.* Ann Arbor, MI: Servant Publications, 2001.

Eckhardt, John. *God Still Speaks: How to Hear and Receive Revelation from God, for Your Family, Church and Community.* Lake Mary, FL: Charisma House Publishing, 2009.

Joyner, Rick. *The Prophetic Ministry.* Wilkesboro, NC: MorningStar Publications, 2003.

McClain, Michelle. *The Prophetic Advantage.* Lake Mary, FL: Charisma House Publishing, 2012.

Swan, David. *The Power of Prophetic Worship: Releasing the Powerful Corporate Anointing and Ushering in the Glory.* Tabernacle of David, 2007.

Prayer, Worship, and Spiritual Warfare

Daniels, Kimberly. *Give It Back! God's Weapons for Turning Evil to Good.* Lake Mary, FL: Charisma House, 2007.

Eckhardt, John. *Prayers That Break Curses.* Lake Mary, FL: Charisma House Publishing, 2010.

Eckhardt, John. *Prayers That Release Heaven on Earth.* Lake Mary, FL: Charisma House Publishing, 2010.

Eckhardt, John. *Prayers That Rout Demons.* Lake Mary, FL: Charisma House Publishing, 2008.

Ing, Richard. *Spiritual Warfare.* New Kensington, PA: Whitaker House, 1996.

Jacobs, Cindy. *Possessing the Gates of Enemy: Training Manual for Militant Intercession.* Grand Rapids, MI: Chosen Books, 2006.

Jacobs, Cindy. *The Power of Persistent Prayer: Praying with Great Purpose and Passion*. Bloomington, MN: Bethany House Publishing, 2010.

Pierce, D. Chuck, and John Dickson. *The Worship Warrior*. Ventura, CA: Regal Books, 2002.

Wagner, Peter C. *Confronting the Queen of Heaven*. Colorado Springs, CO: Wagner Publications, 2001.

Love, Faith in God, Healing, and the Power of God and the Holy Spirit

Baxter, K. Mary, and T. L. Lowery. *The Power of the Blood: Healing for Your Spirit, Soul, and Body*. New Kensington, PA: Whitaker House, 2005.

Chapman, Gary. *The 5 Love Languages: The Secret to Love That Lasts*. Chicago, IL: Northfield Publishing, 2010.

Deere, Jack. *Surprised by the Voice of God*. Grand Rapids, MI: Zondervan Publishing Company, 1996.

Heidler, Robert. *Experiencing the Spirit: Developing a Living Relationship with the Holy Spirit*. Ventura, CA: Renew Books Publishing, 1998.

Prince, Derek. *The Marriage Covenant*. Charlotte, NC: 1978.

Sorger, Matt. *Power for Life: Keys to a Life Marked by the Presence of God*. Lake Mary, FL: Charisma House, 2011.

Sumrall, Lester. *The Names of God: God's Name Brings Hope, Healing, and Happiness*. New Kensington, PA: Whitaker House, 1982.

Swan, Irene. *A Peek into the Father's Heart*. West Malaysia: Tabernacle of David, 2003.

Wigglesworth, Smith. *Ever Increasing Faith: A Legacy of Love and Faith from One of the Great Spiritual Leaders of Modern Times.* Springfield, MI: Gospel Publishing House, 2001.

Wigglesworth, Smith. *Smith Wigglesworth on Healing.* New Kensington, PA: Whitaker House, 1999.

Exposing Spiritual Darkness

Clark, Jonas. *Exposing Spiritual Witchcraft: How to Overcome Curses, Demons, Witchcraft and Controlling Powers.* Hallandale Beach, FL: Spirit of Life Publishing, 2003.

Greenwood, Rebecca. *Let Our Children Go: Steps to Free Your Child from Evil Influences and Demonic Harassment.* Lake Mary, FL: Charisma House Publishing, 2011.

Heidler, Robert. *Set Yourself Free: A Deliverance Manual.* Denton, TX: Glory of Zion Ministries, 2002.

Joyner, Rick. *Delivered from Evil: Preparing for the Age to Come.* Shippensburg, PA: Destiny Image Publishers, 2004.

Pierce, Chuck D., and Rebecca Sytsema Wagner. *Protecting Your Home from Spiritual Darkness.* Ventura, CA: Regal Books, 2004.

Rousse, Drew, and David Alsobrook. *Witch's Brew in the Pew.* Kirkwood, MO: Impact Christian Books, 2000.

Sudduth, William. *What's behind the Ink? The Spiritual Aspects of Tattooing, Piercing, and Other Fads from a Christian Perspective.* Colorado Springs, CO: Righteous Acts Ministries, 2008.

Wagner, C. Peter. *Freedom from the Religious Spirit: Understand How Deceptive Religious Forces Try to Destroy God's Plan and Purpose for His Church.* Ventura, CA: Regal Books, 2005.

Notes

Biblegateway.com, "Amplified Bible," http://www.Biblegateway.com/passage/ (accessed June 10, 2011).

Collins English Dictionary—Complete and Unabridged © HarperCollins Publishers 1991, 1994, 1998, 2000, 2003, (accessed April 8, 2011).

en.wiktionary.org/wiki/effeminate (accessed April 8, 2011).

Freedictionary.com, http://www.thefreedictionary.com/invincible (accessed April 8, 2011).

Merriam Webster's Dictionary, http://www.wordcentral.com/cgi-bin/student_clean?va=nice (accessed April 8, 2011).

About IFOC

Interceding for Our Children (IFOC) is a nonprofit 501(c)(3) organization. There is a war going on against our innocent children. If we don't stand up and fight back with our spiritual armor, this war on innocent unborn babies and young children will continue to increase. The purpose of IFOC is to sound the alarm that we, the pro-life citizens of the United States of America, are furious about the heinous crimes against our innocent children.

Crimes by any and all abortion procedures, including the day-after pill, violent shootings in our schools, and children being released in custody battles or visitation rights to mentally unstable parents, lead to innocent children's deaths. We are no longer going to tolerate the government's passive response of action to such heinous crimes. This is a great injustice to our children, the next generation. Interceding for Our Children (IFOC)—with the help from other supporters—will stand in the gap to pray and fight for what's right. Let God back into the schools. Put an end to violent shootings in our schools and abortions. Our children need God, and our nation needs God!

Purpose

There is a war going on against innocent children. The purpose of IFOC is to protect innocent children from heinous crimes, such as violent shootings in our schools, abortion procedures, and children being released in custody battles or visitation rights to mentally unstable parents, which leads to innocent children's deaths.

Mission

Some people think a child's life is insignificant, but those people don't know who the baby, young child, or children really are. All children are created for a purpose and are on earth for a God-given reason!

IFOC—with the help of other supporters—will stand in the gap to pray and fight for what's right. Let God back in the school, provide physical protection, and put an end to abortion. Our children need God, and our nation needs God!

To get our youth involved in supporting the importance of protecting and defending the life of a child.

To get people involved by contacting their state representatives, starting petitions, having the petitions signed, and sending them to Congress. This will send a clear message that we want prayer back in our schools. We want law enforcement to provide protection for our children on school campuses. We want abortion clinics, abortion procedures, and all other forms of abortion to be illegal and shut down.

To launch up a network of intercessors in every state (prayer teams) to assemble worship and prayer walks around and inside school campuses, abortion clinics, and all forms of organizations that perform abortion procedures.

We must understand the thrones that God desires us to occupy. Right now, there are thrones that principalities sit on. The principalities from these thrones determine what society and culture look like. We must remove them from these thrones, and the ecclesia (the Church) must take its place so we can become the ruling entity over cities, regions, and territories. We, as true Holy Spirit-filled believers, have individual thrones to sit in and govern from (Colossians 1:16).

"And has raised us up together, and made us sit together in heavenly places in Christ Jesus" (Ephesians 2:6).

There are three dimensions we can live our lives and function from.

- the anointing level (Isaiah 10: 27)
- the second level of life is from authority (Matthew 10:1–2)
- the third level of life and ministry is the throne level or seat of government (Proverbs 20:8)

Believers of Christ Jesus can gather up other believers (God's warriors) and assign prayer teams to execute prayer walks around local schools at least one or two times per week when possible. Church ministries could call local schools to inquire about whether they can submit a use-of-facility form (this form will allow ministries to access school property and the ability to use a classroom or other rooms for a small reasonable fee). This is an entry gate for prayer teams.

Living stones are not limited to a designated church building where we assemble on certain days of the week. We are the living church (living stones).

As a believer and American citizen, you should start a petition in your state. Call your congressman, state representative, or mayor. We can make a great difference!

Here is an example that can be modified. This can be effective by true faith and worship.

Each prayer team should have at least two intercessors to lead the prayer team along with five to ten other prayer warriors. This number may vary. Jesus said where two or three gather in his name, he will be in the midst of them.

We also know that more prayer and faith equals more power. Having more prayer warriors on a team is awesome. Intercessors can provide a vital leading position in spiritual warfare. Intercessors are mediators on behalf of those who cannot intervene or fight for themselves. Any person can pray, but not all praying people are intercessors.

If a church ministry is lacking intercessors, seek out other strong, mature individuals in the Lord to lead the prayer team. We can agree to stand in the gap and intercede on behalf of another person or situation. Since every state and region has a different climate, please pray for spiritual strategies when going about this assignment. When interceding, remember to ask God about the legal grounds that the enemy have in your state, city, or region that give openings for demonic oppression.

When interceding, create an atmosphere of worship by singing songs of praise and worship for at least forty-five minutes. Follow this with prayers and the Holy Spirit. Each person on the prayer team should be able to release words of God's divine protection, healing, forgiveness, peace, and Jesus Christ's saving power through his blood. Allow the Holy Spirit to move freely so that all spiritual gifts can flow fully and freely.

When creating an atmosphere of worship and prayer, darkness must flee. We can dismantle the spirit of death, murder, destruction, fear, and hate that is against the unborn fetus, young children, preteens, and teens throughout our nation.

For more information, email us at rebekahkingdom9@gmail.com, or (808) 265-7815.

Visit us at www.intercedingforourchildren.net or www.facebook.com/kingdomIFOC

www.ingramcontent.com/pod-product-compliance
Lightning Source LLC
Chambersburg PA
CBHW060848050426
42453CB00008B/896